EGMONT
We bring stories to life

First published in Great Britain in 2020 by Egmont Books UK Ltd
2 Minster Court, 10th floor, London EC3R 7BB
www.egmontbooks.co.uk

Written by Laura Jackson
Designed by Jeannette O'Toole with Ruby Shoes Limited

Parental guidance is advised for all craft and colouring activities. Always ask an adult to help when using glue, paint and scissors. Wear protective clothing and cover surfaces to avoid staining.

Stay safe online. Egmont is not responsible for content hosted by third parties.

Egmont takes its responsibility to the planet and its inhabitants very seriously. We aim to use papers from well-managed forests run by responsible suppliers.

ISBN 978 1 4052 9645 8
70842/003
Printed in Italy

Disney

FROZEN

Annual 2021

belongs to ....

....

Contents

Frozen Friends 8

Snowy Style 10

Build a Snowman 11

Find the Troll 12

STORY: Queen for a Day 14

Festive Fun 20

Adventure Awaits 21

Are You Anna or Elsa? 22

Winter Wonders 24

Troll Wisdom 25

Whirling Snowstorm 26

STORY: The Perfect Game 28

Love is All Around 32

Posters 33

Friends Forever 35

Believe in Yourself 36

Posters 37

New Beginnings 39

New Friends	40
STORY: *Frozen 2*	42
Enchanted Forest	48
Magic Mist	50
Boom, Boom, Boom!	51
Swirling Colours	52
Odd One Out	53
STORY: *Frozen 2*	54
Magic Memory	58
Counting Challenge	59
Double Act	60
Peace and Harmony	61
Ice Crash	62
Nature Hunt	63
A Big Surprise	64
Deep, Dark Sea	65
Nature Spirits	66
Together	68
Answers	69

Frozen Friends

Meet the Arendelle friends who bring adventure, love and friendship to life!

Elsa

Elsa was born with the power to create ice and snow. For years she kept her magic a secret from the world – even from her sister. When her powers are revealed, Elsa can finally set her magic free.

Anna

Anna is Elsa's younger sister. Unlike Elsa, Anna shares all of her feelings. She has a big heart and loves her sister more than anything. Anna hates sitting around and loves to jump from adventure to adventure.

Kristoff and Sven

Kristoff was brought up by trolls in the mountains and he loves being outdoors with his reindeer, Sven. He might look tough, but inside he is kind and soft – especially when it comes to Anna!

Olaf

Olaf is a happy little snowman who just loves a hug! He can't leave his cold mountain in the summer in case he melts. But when Elsa makes him his own snow cloud, all his sunny dreams can come true.

Snowy Style

Brrrr! Anna is getting ready for an adventure, but it is cold outside. Colour in her outfit, then design some accessories to keep her warm.

gloves

scarf

hat

10

Build a Snowman

Whee! Olaf loves to go rolling in the snow, but he keeps falling apart.

Use a pencil to draw Olaf in one piece again.

11

Find the Troll

A young troll is missing and Anna, Elsa, Kristoff and Olaf are searching for him. Play this fun board game to see who'll be the first one to find him.

HOW TO PLAY

Up to four people can play this game. Use coins as counters and place one on each character. Then take turns to throw a dice and move the number of spaces shown.

TROLL

If you land on a troll MOVE FORWARD 1 SPACE.

ROCK

If you land on a rock GO BACK 1 SPACE.

The first player to reach the lost troll wins!

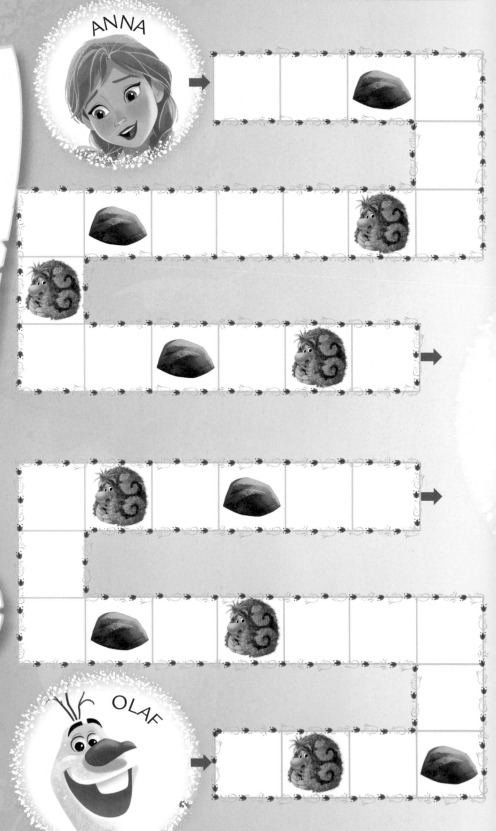

KRISTOFF

ELSA

13

Queen for a Day

ELSA IS GOING ON A BUSINESS TRIP TO LICHEN FARMS, AND ANNA WILL BE IN CHARGE FOR THE DAY ...

WHAT IF I DON'T KNOW WHAT I HAVE TO DO?

I TRUST YOU. YOU'LL DO JUST FINE...

BUT IN CASE YOU NEED ADVICE, HERE ARE SOME LITTLE TIPS.

THANKS! I THINK I'LL NEED THEM.

WISH ME LUCK!

YOU'LL BE GREAT! SEE YOU TOMORROW!

OK, I'LL START BY READING ELSA'S LETTER.

EXCUSE ME, YOUR HIGHNESS, YOU'RE NEEDED IN **THE THRONE ROOM.**

Script: Tea Orsi; Layout: Emilio Urbano; Cleanup: Manuela Razzi; Colour: Stefania Santi

WHAT IF YOU LET THE CHICKENS EAT THE CORN AND THE COWS EAT THE GRASS? AND YOU CAN SHARE THE MILK AND EGGS!

THAT'S A GOOD SOLUTION!

THAT COULD BE ...

WE'LL DO AS PRINCESS ANNA SUGGESTS!

PARDON ME, YOUR HIGHNESS ...

THE ARENDELLE ROWING TEAM IS ONE PERSON SHORT. THEY MIGHT NOT BE ABLE TO COMPETE IN THE **ROYAL REGATTA!**

OH NO! THERE'S NO TIME TO WASTE.

HMMM... ELSA WROTE, "DON'T BE AFRAID **TO MIX IT UP"**!

I'VE GOT IT! I'LL HELP THE TEAM!

SO ...

WE CAN DO IT! WE'RE NEARLY THERE!

SPLISH

SPLOSH

WE WON!

GOOD JOB, TEAM ARENDELLE! **SECOND** PLACE IS OURS!

HURRAH FOR PRINCESS ANNA!

AFTER THE RACE, IT'S TIME FOR A VISIT TO THE VILLAGE SCHOOL ...

MY SISTER, ELSA, SUGGESTED MIXING IN SOME FUN WITH THE WORK. SO ...

WHO WANTS TO PLAY HIDE AND SEEK? I BET I CAN CATCH YOU ALL!

THEN THERE ARE THE INVITATIONS TO THE ANNUAL BALL TO BE SIGNED ...

SCRITT SCRITT

THE ROYAL TROOPS NEED TO BE INSPECTED ...

NOW YOUR UNIFORM IS SPOTLESS!

... AND THE BOAT RACE AWARD CEREMONY HAS TO BE ATTENDED!

I'M SO HAPPY TO MEET YOU!

HUH?

Festive Fun

Elsa has created an ice rink for the people of Arendelle. Can you spot the close-ups in the big picture?

Answers on page 69

Adventure Awaits

Olaf is ready for an adventure. But he keeps spinning around in the ice and now he is dizzy and lost. Guide Olaf through the slippery maze to Kristoff and Sven so their adventure can begin.

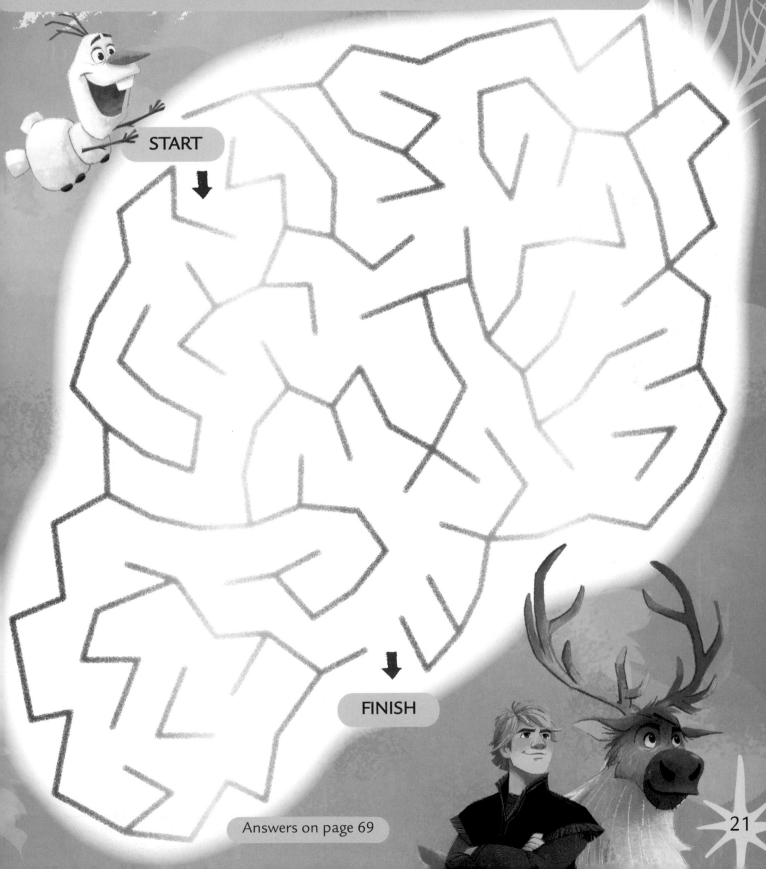

START

FINISH

Answers on page 69

21

Are you Anna or Elsa?

Which sister are you most like?
Take the quiz to find out.

1

What is your favourite way to celebrate your birthday?

a A quiet meal with a few friends.

b A big party with lots of dancing.

2

If you have a problem, what do you do?

a Try to solve it yourself.

b Tell your friends and family to see if they can help.

3

Which words describe you best?

a Calm, caring and shy.

b Loving, fun and busy, busy, busy!

4

What colour clothes do you like to wear?

a Icy blue, silver and white.

b Green, purple and blue.

5

What do you like to do for fun?

a Be outside in nature.

b Hang out with friends and family.

6

Are you good at keeping secrets?

a Yes, you never tell.

b Erm, not always!

7

If you were Queen for the day, what would you do?

a Make sure everybody was happy.

b Throw a big party for everyone.

MOSTLY a
YOU ARE ELSA!
Shy but strong, you often put other people before yourself. But when you believe in yourself, amazing things can happen.

MOSTLY b
YOU ARE ANNA!
From throwing parties to sharing secrets, you are happiest with friends and family. You have a big heart and are always ready for the next crazy adventure.

Winter Wonders

Elsa can create snow and ice palaces with her magical powers. Dream up a towering ice building and draw it below.

Will it have windows and doors?

Who will live there?

Troll Wisdom

Grand Pabbie is the wisest friend in Arendelle. Show him how smart you are by spotting five differences in the second picture.

a

b

Answers on page 69

Whirling Snowstorm

Anna has raced ahead to find a route to Elsa's ice palace. But a fierce snowstorm has surrounded her friends. Quickly guide Sven, Olaf and Kristoff through the storm to catch up with Anna.

START →

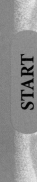

FINISH

The Perfect Game

ANNA AND ELSA HAVE INVITED THE TOWNSPEOPLE TO JOIN THEM TOMORROW FOR A TRADITIONAL PARTY ...

NO, NO. THIS WON'T WORK, EITHER!

ELSA, YOU SEEM SO STRESSED. WHAT'S WRONG?

I'D LIKE TO ORGANISE SOMETHING **SPECIAL** TO ENTERTAIN OUR GUESTS. SOMETHING NEW AND **EXCITING** BUT ALSO INSPIRED BY OUR TRADITIONS.

AND ALL THE IDEAS I'VE COME UP WITH SO FAR **DON'T** QUITE WORK!

I KNOW WHAT TO DO! FOLLOW ME!

Original story by Erica David; Adapted by Tea Orsi; Layout: Alberto Zanon; Clean-Up: Nicoletta Baldari; Colour: Dario Calabria

28

WHAT DID YOU WANT TO SHOW ME?

NOTHING! I JUST THOUGHT THAT YOU NEEDED A **REFRESHING BREAK** TO FIND THE RIGHT IDEA, SO ...

SPLAT

... WHAT'S BETTER THAN **SNOWBALLS**?

A SNOWBALL FIGHT THEN?!

MAY THE BEST WIN!

SWOOOSH

HAHA! TRY AGAIN!

Love is all Around

Anna loves her sister, her friends, having adventures and dancing! Draw some people and things that you love inside the snowball.

You could draw your family, something you love to do or your favourite sweet treat.

TRUE
to Myself

Find Your
STRENGTH

Friends Forever

Magic is in the air! Use your crayons to add colour to this picture of Anna and Elsa. You could add glitter on the snowballs too!

Believe in Yourself

When Elsa believes in herself, she can do amazing things.
Use a pencil to trace over these words all about Elsa.

snow

strong

brave

kind

STRONGER
Together

New Beginnings

Anna and Elsa have been living peacefully in Arendelle. But when Elsa hears a voice calling her to the Enchanted Forest, they know their lives are about to change.

Use your crayons to colour in this picture before Anna and Elsa set off on their new journey.

New Friends

Far beyond Arendelle, Anna and Elsa are about to meet a whole new world of friends.

Honeymaren longs to be free and escape the spells of the Enchanted Forest. She is bold and brave and is always ready to stick up for herself.

Honeymaren

Ryder

Honeymaren's brother loves reindeer and being outdoors, just like Kristoff. The pair make fast friends and Ryder even shows Kristoff how to propose to Anna – reindeer style!

Yelana

As the leader of the Northuldra, Yelana is protective of her people. Nature is everything to her. If people listen to the signs of nature, she will take them into her group.

Mattias has been trapped in the Enchanted Forest for thirty years. He was King Agnarr's guard and has never forgotten his duty to Arendelle.

Mattias

Wind Spirit

Gale is full of mischief. He spins and whirls to create a vortex of wind and power.

Fire Spirit

Bruni is a salamander who sparks fires when things go wrong. Only Elsa can calm him and make his flames go out.

Earth Spirit

These powerful giants can look like hills and mountains when they are asleep. But when they wake, they make the ground shake. BOOM!

Water Spirit

The Water Nokk is a warrior who guards the secrets of the forest. Only the bravest dare to pass it in the water.

DISNEY FROZEN II

In Arendelle, long ago …

King Agnarr told his daughters a story about the people of Northuldra. They lived peacefully with the spirits of nature. But when the Arendelliens and the Northuldra fell out, a mist trapped them in the Enchanted Forest.

Many years later …

Elsa heard a strange voice calling to her. She blasted ice into the air and it transformed into a forest – the Enchanted Forest from King Agnarr's stories!

Ice crystals hung in the air and then dropped from the sky.

Arendelle transformed. Water stopped flowing, fires went out and wind drove people from their houses.

Elsa's magic had woken something up. **"The spirits of nature are awake,** and they are still very angry," Grand Pabbie told her.

Elsa knew she had to follow the voice to the Enchanted Forest, but Anna wouldn't let her go alone.

So Anna, Elsa, Olaf, Sven and Kristoff set off together. They travelled North, into the unknown.

At last, they reached a glittering wall of mist. **The Enchanted Forest!**

As the mist parted, the friends stepped forward. A gust of wind blasted them into the air. It was the **Wind Spirit.**

Elsa quickly threw out snow and ice into the centre of the whirlwind.

Suddenly, people appeared from the trees. It was the Northuldra and the Arendelliens from King Agnarr's story!

Elsa used her magic, shocking everyone into silence.

45

Elsa turned to the people and asked for their trust to free them. "We only trust nature," said Yelana, the leader of the Northuldra.

The two sides began to argue.

As Elsa tried to make peace, fire bolts whooshed through the forest. It was the **Fire Spirit.** Elsa blasted out ice and snow.

But when Elsa caught up to the Fire Spirit, it was not what she had expected. It was a tiny salamander!

Elsa then spoke to the people of the forest: **"I promise you, I will free this forest and restore Arendelle."**

A girl called Honeymaren noticed the spirit pictures on Elsa's scarf. There was a FIFTH SPIRIT, called the **bridge.** It connected magic to humans.

Elsa knew she had to journey further North to unravel the secrets of the past and Anna and Olaf were right by her side.

The story continues on page 54.

47

Enchanted Forest

The forest is full of ancient magic and spells. Are you ready to help the friends across the enchanted land to reach Elsa?

HOW TO PLAY:

✷ Each player picks a friend to guide through the forest.

✷ Place your counters on the start.

✷ Then take turns to roll the dice and move the number of spaces shown.

✷ Follow the instructions along the way.

✷ The first player to reach Elsa wins!

Anna

Olaf

Ryder

Honeymaren

YOU WILL NEED:
- 2-4 players
- a dice
- counters – you could use coins or bits of paper

START

1

2 The **FIRE SPIRIT** sparks a fire. RUN FORWARD 2 SPACES

3 **EARTH GIANTS** shake the ground. MISS A GO

4

5 The **MIST** pushes you forward. GO FORWARD 3 SPACES

6

7 Hop on an **ICE BOAT** and take a SHORT CUT

8

9 You get stuck in the **WIND SPIRIT**'s blast. GO BACK 2 SPACES

10

11 The **FIRE SPIRIT** sparks a fire. RUN FORWARD 2 SPACES

12

13

19

20

The **FIRE SPIRIT** sparks a fire. RUN FORWARD 2 SPACES

Elsa

18

Hop on an **ICE BOAT** and take a SHORT CUT

21

30

FINISH

17

EARTH GIANTS shake the ground. MISS A GO

22

29

EARTH GIANTS shake the ground. MISS A GO

16

The **MIST** pushes you forward. GO FORWARD 3 SPACES

23

28

15

24

Hop on an **ICE BOAT** and take a SHORT CUT

27

14

You get stuck in the **WIND SPIRIT's** blast. GO BACK 2 SPACES

25

26

The **FIRE SPIRIT** sparks a fire. RUN FORWARD 2 SPACES

Magic Mist

A glittering mist surrounds the Enchanted Forest.

Can you tick ✔ the friends below that are hidden in the haze?

1 ⬜ 2 ✓ 3 ⬜ 4 ✓ 5 ✓

Answers on page 69

Boom, Boom, Boom!

QUICK! Olaf has woken up the Earth Giants.
You have 20 seconds to find the safe path back
to Ryder and Kristoff. Set a timer, then … **run!**

c

b

a

Answers on page 69

Swirling Colours

A strange wind surrounds Anna. It's the Wind Spirit! Use your crayons to bring the magic to life.

Odd One Out

These pictures of Honeymaren and Ryder look the same, but one is different. Can you spot the odd one out?

c

a

b

f

d

e

Answers on page 69

DISNEY
FROZEN II

continued from page 47 ...

Anna, Elsa and Olaf walked on and on, until they saw something in the distance. A shipwreck. Anna and Elsa gasped. It was their parents' ship!

Anna found a map in the cabin. The map showed that their parents had crashed when they were heading to Ahtohallan, to seek answers to Elsa's magic.

"This is my fault!" said Elsa, tears streaming down her face. "If anyone can free the forest, it's you," said Anna.

Elsa knew she had to carry on – but she needed to do it alone. "No," said Anna. **"We do this together. I can't lose you."**

But Elsa had made up her mind. It was too dangerous for Anna. So she blasted out a stream of ice ...

... and magically created an ice boat under Anna and Olaf. WHOOSH!

Elsa journeyed on alone, until she reached the Dark Sea. Giant waves crashed and rumbled.

With a deep breath, Elsa ran into the water. Snowflakes formed under her feet. She came face to face with the mighty **Water Nokk**. It stared deep into Elsa's eyes.

The pair started a fierce battle. Elsa shot out ice blasts, but the Water Nokk shattered the ice.

The battle raged on until Elsa created an ice bridle and jumped on top of the spirit. The Water Spirit finally became calm.

Elsa felt calm too and at peace. She was now sure that harmony could be restored in the forest and in Arendelle.

Meanwhile, Elsa and Olaf were quietly rowing past the snoring Earth Giants. "They're huge!" said Olaf.

As they found safety in a dark cavern, an ice sculpture appeared. It showed that Elsa had made it across the Dark Sea.

The ice also revealed secrets of the forest. At that moment, Anna knew she could help to free the people.

Anna was ready for anything.

The End

Magic Memory

Now take the quiz to see how much you remember about the story.

1 Who told Anna and Elsa the story of the Northuldra?

a OLAF   **b** KRISTOFF   **c** KING AGNARR

2 Who hears a voice calling them to the Enchanted Forest?

a ANNA   **b** ELSA   **c** OLAF

3 What is trapping people in the Enchanted Forest?

a MIST   **b** ICE   **c** FIRE

4 Who is the leader of the Northuldra?

a YELANA   **b** RYDER   **c** FIRE SPIRIT

5 What spirit is under the Dark Sea?

a FIRE SPIRIT   **b** WATER NOKK   **c** EARTH GIANTS

Answers on page 69

Counting Challenge

Honeymaren lives among the spirits of nature.
How many leaves are whirling in the forest today?

I can
count

leaves.

Do you know which spirit creates blustery winds?

Answers on page 69

Double Act

Anna never likes Elsa to be too far away! Draw a line to link up the only matching pair of pictures below.

Answers on page 69

Peace and Harmony

When the Northuldra and the Arendelliens argue, Elsa tries to help them make friends. Can you circle all the kind words and cross out all the unkind words?

peace

battle

happy

enemy

friend

kind

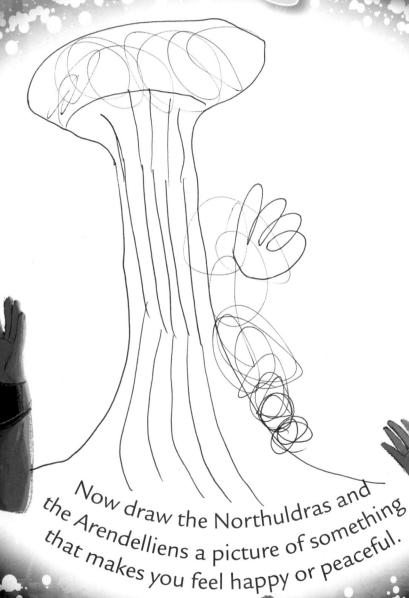

Now draw the Northuldras and the Arendelliens a picture of something that makes you feel happy or peaceful.

Ice Crash

Whoosh! Anna and Olaf are speeding down an ice path. Pick a path, grab a pencil and race down the path to the end. If you crash into the sides, start again!

1
2
3

Then challenge a friend to see if they can race to the end without crashing, too.

Nature Hunt

Yelana listens to the nature all around her. Next time you go outside, take this checklist with you and see how many you can see.

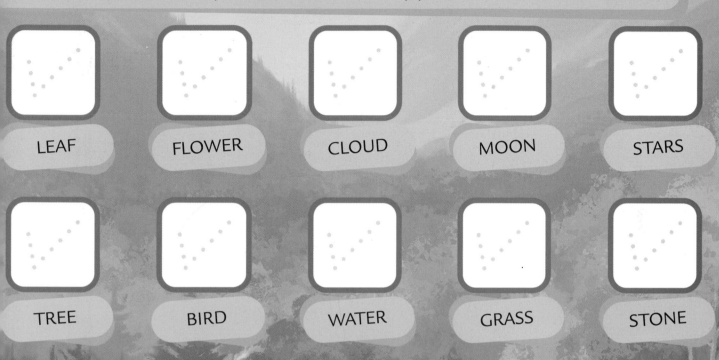

| LEAF | FLOWER | CLOUD | MOON | STARS |

| TREE | BIRD | WATER | GRASS | STONE |

Draw the most interesting things you saw on your journey into nature.

A Big Surprise

Kristoff wants to ask Anna to marry him. If only he could keep up with her! Follow the directions shown to find the route to Anna.

START →

FINISH

Answers on page 69

Deep, Dark Sea

Elsa has to cross the Dark Sea. Imagine
what creatures might be in the water
and draw them under the waves.

Nature Spirits

Match up the descriptions below to the nature spirits.

1
This cheeky spirit loves to create a storm and send people into a spin.

2
A warrior who guards the secrets of the forest. Beware of its power in the Dark Sea.

3
If you wake up this grumpy spirit, the earth will tremble and shake!

4
This fiery spirit can cause destruction. But Elsa knows how to cool it down.

a

b

c

d

66

Answers on page 69

Now dream up your own amazing **nature spirit**.
It could be a spirit of the SKY, a spirit of RAINBOWS,
a spirit of STORMS or a spirit of FLOWERS.

- Will it have WINGS?
- Will it be CUTE or FIERCE?
- Will it be BIG or SMALL?

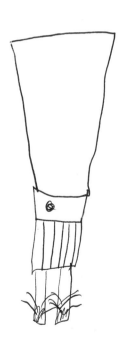

SPIRIT NAME _Soow_

POWER _Ice_

Together

Answers

PAGE 20 *Festive Fun*

PAGE 21 *Adventure Awaits*

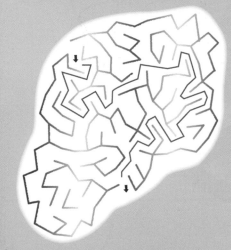

PAGE 25 *Troll Wisdom*

PAGE 26 *Whirling Snowstorm*

PAGE 50 *Magic Mist*

Pictures 2, 4 and 5 are hidden in the mist

PAGE 51 *Boom, Boom, Boom!*

Path **a** leads to Ryder and Kristoff

PAGE 53 *Odd One Out*

Picture **c** is the odd one out

PAGE 58 *Magic Memory*

1. **c** – King Agnarr
2. **b** – Elsa
3. **a** – mist
4. **a** – Yelana
5. **b** – Water Nokk

PAGE 59 *Counting Challenge*

I can count 11 leaves
The wind spirit creates blustery winds

PAGE 60 *Double Act*

3 and 4 are matching pairs

PAGE 64 *A Big Surprise*

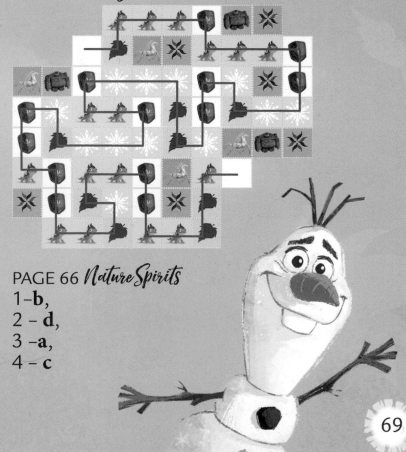

PAGE 66 *Nature Spirits*

1–**b**,
2 – **d**,
3 –**a**,
4 – **c**